The Hidden Child
Kids with Autism

Kids with Special Needs

The Hidden Child

Kids with Autism

by Sheila Stewart and Camden Flath

MASON CREST PUBLISHERS INC.
370 Reed Road
Broomall, Pennsylvania 19008
(866)MCP-BOOK (toll free)
www.masoncrest.com

First Printing
9 8 7 6 5 4 3 2 1

ISBN (set) 978-1-4222-1727-6   ISBN (pbk set) 978-1-4222-1918-8

Library of Congress Cataloging-in-Publication Data

Stewart, Sheila, 1975–
  The hidden child : kids with autism / by Sheila Stewart and Camden Flath.
     p. cm.
  Includes bibliographical references and index.
  ISBN 978-1-4222-1724-5   ISBN (pbk) 978-1-4222-1927-0
  1. Autism in children—Juvenile literature. I. Flath, Camden, 1987– II. Title.
  RJ506.A9S743 2010
  618.92'85882—dc22
                    2010007064

Produced by Harding House Publishing Service, Inc.
www.hardinghousepages.com
Design by MK Bassett-Harvey.
Cover design by Torque Advertising Design.
Printed in the USA by Bang Printing.

Photo Credits
Creative Commons Attribution 2.0 Generic: fallenangel_brokenwings: p. 32;
Fotolia: Arcurs, Yuri: p. 36; GNU Free Documentation License, Version 1.2:
Vickers, Tim: p. 27; United States Army: pp. 30, 38, 41, 43.

The creators of this book have made every effort to provide accurate information, but it should not be used as a substitute for the help and services of trained professionals.

Introduction

To the Teacher

Kids with Special Needs provides a unique forum for demystifying a wide variety of childhood medical and developmental disabilities. Written to captivate an elementary-level audience, the books bring to life the challenges and triumphs experienced by children with common chronic conditions such as hearing loss, intellectual disability, physical differences, and speech difficulties. The topics are addressed frankly through a blend of fiction and fact.

This series is particularly important today as the number of children with special needs is on the rise. Over the last two decades, advances in pediatric medical techniques have allowed children who have chronic illnesses and disabilities to live longer, more functional lives. At the same time, IDEA, a federal law, guarantees their rights to equal educational opportunities. As a result, these children represent an increasingly visible part of North American population in all aspects of daily life. Students are exposed to peers with special needs in their classrooms, through extracurricular activities, and in the community. Often, young people have misperceptions and unanswered questions about a child's disabilities—and more important, his or her abilities. Many times, there is no vehicle for talking about these complex issues in a comfortable manner.

This series will encourage further conversation about these issues. Most important, the series promotes a greater comfort for its readers as they live, play, and study side by side with these children who have medical and developmental differences—kids with special needs.

—*Dr. Carolyn Bridgemohan*
Boston Pediatric Hospital/Harvard Medical School

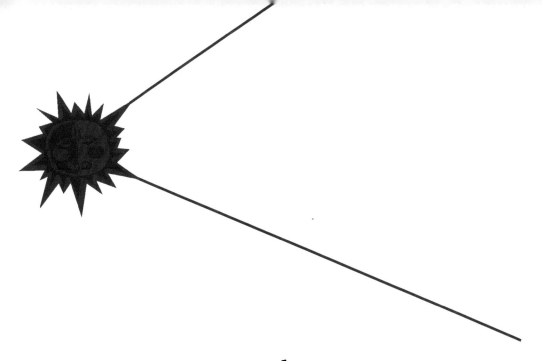

Dog man coming today.

Daniel was excited. He had been counting the days until the man with the search-and-rescue dogs came to talk to his school.

He bounced in the backseat of the car. "Dog man coming," he said. "Dog man coming."

"Sit still, Daniel!" Mama said. She didn't like Daniel to bounce while she was driving.

James, Daniel's twin, reached over and put his hand on Daniel's arm. James always made Daniel feel calmer and better. Daniel thought that was because James had hugged him and comforted him even before they were born.

People said he and James were identical, but Daniel didn't know why. Obviously, James was James and he was Daniel. Nobody ever seemed to get them confused either. James said that was because Daniel had autism and James didn't, but Daniel didn't know if that was really it. It wasn't like people could see his autism. It was inside his head, wasn't it?

"Dog man," Daniel whispered, holding himself very stiff so he didn't bounce. "Dog man, dog man, dog man."

He loved dogs more than anything else in the world. (Except for James, of course.) Every day, after school, he went to the Humane Society and helped take care of the dogs. The people who owned the apartment where he and James and Mama lived wouldn't let them have a dog of their own. He hoped the dog man would bring a lot of dogs with him to school.

Daniel's classroom was noisy that morning. He hated noise. Mama always drove him and James to school, because he hated the noise on the school bus, but there was nothing she could do about the noise in the classroom. He wished James was in his class, but James was in another fifth-grade room across the hall.

Instead of sitting at his desk, Daniel went to his safe spot. Mrs. King the teacher and Mr. Arredondo the aide had made the safe spot just for him. They had told him he could go there whenever he felt anxious and worried. The safe spot was in the very back corner of the room, behind a bookshelf. It had a pillow to sit on and a picture of a border collie on the wall. Daniel sat on the pillow and put his hands over his ears so he couldn't hear the noise outside his safe spot. He hummed to make the noise go away even more, and he rocked his body while he looked at the border collie.

He saw Mr. Arredondo's shadow before he saw Mr. Arredondo, so Daniel took his hands away from his ears. Mr. Arredondo didn't touch him. He had

done that once, and Daniel had started to scream. Daniel didn't like to be touched. Except by James and Mama.

"Too loud in here for you, buddy?" Mr. Arredondo asked.

Daniel didn't think he needed to answer that. "Dog man coming," he said.

"Yep, that's right. We're going to do some math and then start lining up for the assembly."

Daniel couldn't wait.

Math was sometimes hard for Daniel. The numbers didn't always seem to mean anything. The other students could take the numbers and do things to them and not care whether they meant anything or not. At least, that's what it seemed like to Daniel. James said the numbers did mean things, but Daniel always wanted to know what they meant. No one could explain them to him.

Today, the class was working on finding the area of rectangles. They had studied that the year before, too, but Daniel hadn't understood it. He knew he had to measure the short side and the long side of the rectangle and then multiply the two numbers together, but he didn't know why. He thought about the word "area." Area meant a place, like when Mama said his aunts and uncles lived in the area around Seoul, Korea. But he didn't know what that had to do with measuring the sides of rectangles.

Mrs. King was drawing a rectangle on the white board and writing numbers beside it. This rectangle was two feet tall and three feet long. Two times three was six—Daniel knew that—but what did it *mean*? Mrs. King colored in the rectangle and said that it was six feet square. Daniel put his head down on his desk and wrapped his arms around his head. He didn't want to think about rectangles anymore. His wished it was time for the dog man to come.

"Daniel?"

Mr. Arredondo's voice was close to Daniel's head, so he knew Mr. Arredondo must be crouching down beside his desk. Daniel took his arms away from his head but he didn't look up.

"Are you having trouble with math today?" Mr. Arredondo asked. "Or are you just tired of waiting for the assembly?"

Daniel didn't answer. The mention of the assembly distracted him from Mr. Arredondo's question about math. He started thinking about the dog man, until Mr. Arredondo asked him again, "Are you having trouble with math today, Daniel?"

Daniel sighed. "Area is place, not rectangles, not numbers. Don't know why. Why numbers. Why multiply. Don't know why."

"You don't understand about finding the area of a rectangle?"

"There is no why about it," Daniel said.

"There is a why," Mr. Arredondo said. "If you sit up, I'll try to help you understand."

"Okay." Daniel sat up. "Explain."

Mr. Arredondo brought over some little colored cubes and showed Daniel how finding the area could show you how many cubes would be in a rectangle.

"Why should I know?" Daniel asked.

"You could figure out how big the floor of a room is. For example, if you were putting down a tile floor and you wanted to know how many tiles to buy."

Daniel thought about floors for a minute. "Okay," he said finally.

Assemblies were not part of the normal routine, which usually meant they were bad and Daniel didn't like them. This assembly was about dogs, though, so it was okay, although Daniel still felt nervous and unsettled as the class lined up to go to the auditorium. He stood at the back of the line, right behind Gina Richardson, who sometimes told Daniel she was his friend. He wasn't sure what she meant by that, but he didn't mind her being around like he did some people. She wasn't loud, and she didn't do unexpected things that startled him, like throwing things or jumping up quickly.

Mr. Arredondo walked next to Daniel when they left the classroom. Usually, he let Daniel walk by himself with the rest of the class, but he knew Daniel was more likely to get upset when something was out of the ordinary. Having Mr. Arredondo next to him helped Daniel stay calm.

In the auditorium, the fifth graders had to sit in the back. It was always that way, but Daniel didn't like it this time. He wanted to be closer to the front so he could see the dog man better. And the dogs. He sat next to the aisle, beside Gina Richardson. Mr. Arredondo was behind him, and he could see James, sitting in the middle of the row across from him. James was leaning forward and looking at him. He waved at Daniel and grinned, and Daniel waved back.

By the time the assembly finally started, Daniel was rocking in his seat. Gina Richardson tried to put her hand on his arm, but he jerked it away.

Then the dog man came out onto the stage, leading a German Shepherd on a leash. Daniel was disappointed the dog man had only brought one dog, and he was frustrated that he was so far away from the stage. When the dog lay down, he could hardly see it.

The principal introduced the dog man, whose name turned out to be Larry Brown. Larry Brown stood up and starting telling everyone about search-and-rescue dogs and the work he did with them. The dog's name was Cricket, he said.

Daniel leaned forward, listening so intently his whole body was tense.

Then something bad happened. The dog man, Larry Brown, said something wrong.

"Since all dogs are colorblind," Larry Brown said, "they have to rely on their noses, instead of looking for a flash of color in the trees like you or I might do."

But that wasn't true. Daniel knew about dogs, and he knew they weren't colorblind. They might see color differently than people did, but they still saw it.

He sat up and stared at Larry Brown. He was breathing fast and his heart was pounding.

Then Larry Brown said another wrong thing. "A dog's saliva is an antiseptic," he said.

That was too much for Daniel.

"No!" Daniel said loudly, looking up at Larry Brown. "No!"

He stood up, his whole body shaking. "No! Wrong, wrong! Not a real dog man! Wrong. No!"

People turned around to stare at him. He heard them whispering and laughing. Larry Brown stopped talking.

The noise around Daniel got louder. He tried to see James, but there were too many faces.

He had to get out. He turned and ran down the aisle, out of the auditorium. His own feet tripped him and he stumbled, but he kept running. He slammed

into the auditorium doors and fell through them. The noise pushed at him. He tripped again and again, bumped against the walls. He was dizzy, crying.

He wanted to get to his safe place. He hated noise, hated people looking at him. The dog man didn't know about dogs, and the world was bad.

He ran into the classroom, fell over someone's backpack on the floor, and finally made it to his safe place. He curled into a ball on the pillow, put his hands over his head, and rocked his body back and forth. He made noises in his throat, over and over again, loud enough to push away the memory of the other noises that had followed him out of the auditorium.

Somebody touched him and Daniel jumped. He pushed at the person and tried to moved backward, away from him.

"Daniel, it's me! James."

Daniel stopped fighting. He let James hug him, holding him like he had done since before they were born. Daniel tried to stop the noises in his throat, but they kept coming out for a while. He was still breathing hard, and his body was still shaking, but he calmed down as James held him.

"I'm sorry, Daniel," James said, after a long time.

"Dog man was wrong," Daniel said. "Can't be a dog man. Dogs not colorblind. Dog saliva not antiseptic. Can't be a dog man."

"I know," James said. "It's going to be okay."

"Want to go home," Daniel said.

"Why don't you come down to the counselor's office and we'll call your mom," somebody said. Daniel opened his eyes and saw Mr. Arredondo close to him. He had his hand on James' shoulder.

"That's not safe place," Daniel said. "This is a safe place."

"I'll come too," James said.

Because James was going too, Daniel agreed to go to the counselor's office.

The counselor's office had a couch with a blanket on it. The counselor woman said Daniel could sit on the couch, but that seemed too out in the open for him. Instead, he wrapped the blanket around himself and sat on the floor in the little space between the end of the couch and the wall. James sat in front of him with his back to the wall. Daniel felt a little better sitting like this.

"I'll be back in a few minutes," Mr. Arredondo told Daniel, "and then we'll call your mom. You'll be okay here."

"Okay," Daniel said.

"Do you want something to drink?" the counselor woman asked Daniel and James after Mr. Arredondo had left.

Daniel didn't answer. He didn't know the counselor woman, and he didn't want to talk to her.

"We'll take some water," James said, and the counselor woman brought them each a glass of water.

Daniel wrapped his hands around the plastic cup. He waited until James took a drink, and then he sipped at his. The water tasted funny, like dust.

He heard footsteps, and then Mr. Arredondo said, "Daniel."

"Daniel, look," James said.

Daniel pulled himself up so he could see over the couch. Mr. Arredondo stood next to the couch and beside him stood Larry Brown and his dog, Cricket.

Daniel wanted to get out and see the dog, but he didn't want to get too close to Larry Brown. He didn't know what to do.

"Hello, Daniel," Larry Brown said. "Your teacher said you were upset about some mistakes I made in the assembly."

"Wrong," Daniel said, very quietly. "Dogs not colorblind, no antiseptic saliva."

"I'm very sorry, Daniel," Larry Brown said. "I thought those things were true, but after the assembly

I looked them up on the Internet, and I see that I was wrong."

Daniel looked at the dog for a long time

Larry Brown asked, "Would you like to meet Cricket?"

"Yes."

James moved so Daniel could get out of his corner.

Daniel sat down next to Cricket and held out his hand to her. He made sure she was between him and Larry Brown. The dog sniffed Daniel's hand and then licked it. Daniel pushed his fingers gently through her soft fur.

Larry Brown stroked Cricket, too.

James put his hand on Daniel's arm, and Daniel put his head on one side toward his brother. He knew James would understand he was giving him a hug. Then he said, "People make mistakes. Mama said so." He still didn't look at Larry Brown. "It's okay to make mistakes."

"Thank you, Daniel," Larry Brown said. "I'm glad I could meet you today. Cricket is glad too."

Daniel stroked Cricket's head. After a long moment, he said, "Thank you, Larry Brown." He scratched behind Cricket's ears, feeling happier than he had all day.

Kids and Autism

Autism is a disorder that affects how a child plays, talks, and learns. Autism also affects a child's ability to understand the people and things around them. Kids with autism may not be able to speak or understand language the way others do. They might have trouble talking and playing with children their age. Often, children with autism need special care from their parents and teachers. Autism can also change the way a child imagines, preventing him from playing or pretending the way others do. This means that kids with autism also have trouble imagining what others feel like. They also can't

Stacking blocks or other objects is often an early sign of autism in a child.

27

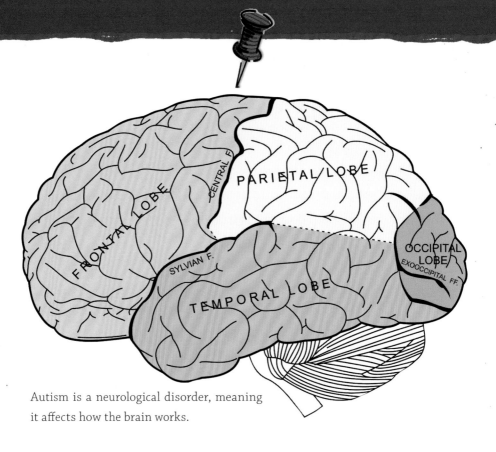

Autism is a neurological disorder, meaning it affects how the brain works.

lie very well! Kids with autism may not be able to imagine what is possible or not real. This can get in the way of their **social** skills, so that it's harder for them to have relationships with others.

Social means having to do with getting along with other people.

Challenges are things that are hard or difficult to handle.

It is important to understand that kids with autism are not bad people—and they may be very intelligent. They simply have to deal with an extra set of difficulties.

The *challenges* presented by autism are great, but there are programs that can help with education, behavior, and social skills.

What Is Autism?

Autism has an impact on the lives of people from every country around the world. It affects people from many different *cultural*, *ethnic*, and *economic* backgrounds.

Autism is a *neurological disorder* that affects the brain early in a child's development. Autism is known as a *spectrum* disorder, which means that each person with autism not only has different symptoms but also different degrees of each symptom. For instance, some children with autism may speak without emotion while some cannot speak at all, and others may use only a few words at a time. While some children with autism are able to go to school and make friends, others

Cultural has to do with a group's customs, traditions, arts, and behaviors.

Ethnic has to do with large groups of people that are connected by language, religion, nationality, or culture.

Economic has to do with money or wealth.

Neurological means having to do with the nerve or brain cells.

A *disorder* is something that doesn't work right.

A *spectrum* is a range in degrees.

Autism has a wide range of symptoms, which is why it is known as a spectrum disorder. Some children with autism need more care than others.

cannot care for themselves and need their parents' help to even dress themselves. Each person with autism has a different set of abilities and behaviors, and each person with autism is affected by the disorder differently.

Here are a few more facts about autism:

- Almost one of every 110 children has some form of autism.
- In the United States, around 1.5 million people have some form of autism.

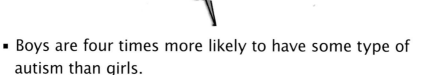

- Boys are four times more likely to have some type of autism than girls.
- Autism is not caused by emotional or **psychological** problems.

Because autism is a spectrum disorder that covers a wide range of conditions, there are both high- and low-functioning forms of autism. Someone who is high-functioning might not even realize she has autism. She might know she has a hard time understanding other people or making friends but not know why. A person who is low-functioning may not be able to speak or take care of herself at all.

> *Psychological means having to do with the mind or the emotions.*

Asperger's Disorder

Another form of autism is called Asperger's disorder. (The disorder is named after Hans Asperger, an Austrian doctor who first described it in 1944.) People with Asperger's also have problems with communication, language, and social skills, but they usually develop language skills at the same age as most other children.

A person with Asperger's usually has trouble making friends. Kids his own age may think he acts strangely,

Kids with Asperger's may seem to act strangely because they do not always understand facial expressions.

and he may not be able to understand what a smile or a frown means. He may be able to speak using the same words as anyone else would, but the tone of his voice may sound flat or strange. He is often very clumsy. Kids with Asperger's are often very interested in one thing, often something that few other kids their age care about (for example, trains, door knobs, historical dates, or lists of numbers). Children with autism are very similar to those with Asperger's disorder, but children with Asperger's are usually able to get along better at school and home.

Autism Behaviors

Children are most likely to first show the behaviors that are linked to autism between the ages of one and three. Because autism is spectrum disorder, the symptoms of autism can be different for each child, and each child with autism may behave differently.

A child with autism may:

- dislike or be unable to deal with change.
- have difficulty in expressing her wants or needs with words.
- repeat words or phrases when speaking with another person.
- like being alone or away from others.
- not respond to being called by name.
- act out or throw tantrums.
- dislike being touched, hugged, or held.
- have difficulty making friends and playing with other children.
- not make eye contact.
- ignore people or events around her.
- be very physically active or not active at all.
- be very sensitive to pain, or not sensitive at all, causing her to act out.

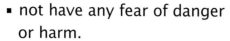

- not have any fear of danger or harm.
- be very clumsy and have a hard time holding a pencil or using scissors.
- react to sounds, sights, and feelings in an unusual or unexpected way.

Many medical risks and problems go along with autism. These can include the risk of **seizures** and mental and emotional disorders. Some children with autism also have **intellectual disabilities**. Many children with autism have **mood disorders** or **anxiety**. Because children with autism are clumsy and they often may not be aware that they are taking risks, they have a higher chance of hurting themselves. Going to the doctor or dentist can be hard

Seizures are sudden electrical activity in the brain that can cause violent shaking, pain, and loss of consciousness.

When people have intellectual disabilities, they have a harder time learning and understanding than other people do. Like autism, intellectual disabilities can be mild, severe, or profound.

People who have mood disorders feel so sad that they are often unable to handle their feelings. Sometimes, they can also feel so excited and happy that they can't control the way they act.

Anxiety is an emotional disorder where someone feels worried and scared almost all the time.

for these children because they do not handle change, pain, or discomfort easily.

What Causes Autism?

There is no single definite cause of autism. *Researchers* are studying a range of possible causes for autism. For example, scientists have taken pictures of the brains of those with autism and seen that there are differences between the average brain and the autistic brain. Other scientists are looking into the possible *genetic* causes of autism. Many medical problems, including autism, may be passed from parents to their children. Some studies seem to show that people are more likely to have autism if they have others in their family with autism too. Scientists also believe that sometimes things (such as certain chemicals) in the environment may trigger autism. Probably a combination of things cause

Researchers are people who study and do experiments in order to find out answers to problems.

Genetic means having to do with genes, the "blueprint" or map inside our bodies' cells, which is passed down from parents to their children, carrying the directions for who we are and what we look like.

autism—and the combination is different from child to child.

Many people around the world are searching hard for the cause of autism. They believe that finding the cause of autism could lead to new treatments or even a cure. Governments have given millions of dollars to autism research, testing, and ***early-intervention programs***.

Early-intervention programs **work to make a difference in a child's life by teaching him when he is still very young the special skills he will need to handle his challenges.**

To be diagnosed with autism, a child must see many different doctors. There is no simple test for the disorder.

Though no specific cause has been found as of yet, the search continues, with experts working together to solve this mysterious disorder.

How Is Autism Diagnosed?

There is no medical test that can be done to check for autism. Instead, a variety of *specialists* and experts must speak with a child and her family, observe the child's behavior, and consider the child's development in comparison with other children's. Among the experts that help to *diagnose* autism and other developmental disorders are speech and hearing specialists, *neurologists*, and *developmental* specialists.

Diagnosing autism as early as possible is important. A diagnosis is the first step to treatment and special services that can help a child with autism.

Specialists are doctors who focus on one type of medicine or one part of the body.

To *diagnose* means to figure out what is wrong with someone.

Neurologists are doctors who specialize in the disorders of the brain and nervous system.

Developmental has to do with how children grow.

Treating Autism

Treatment for children with autism includes teaching them how to communicate and get along with others. Basic daily living skills—like how to get dressed, go the bathroom, or brush their teeth—can also help children with autism get

School is likely to be a challenge for a child with autism, but he can still excel in some areas, like art.

along at home better. Oftentimes, children with autism will have speech and language **therapy**. Speech and language experts can help kids with autism link words to their meaning, understand correct language usage, and improve their ability to speak. School is usually a very important part of autism treatment. Most school-age children with autism will receive most of their treatment program at school.

Autism and School

Once a school **classifies** a child as having autism, the school will begin making changes in the child's education. Since autism covers such a wide range of challenges, there are also many different kinds of changes a child might need. These range from working with a special teacher who is trained to understand autism to having an aide who helps the child get along in a regular classroom. Many times, a child with autism can learn

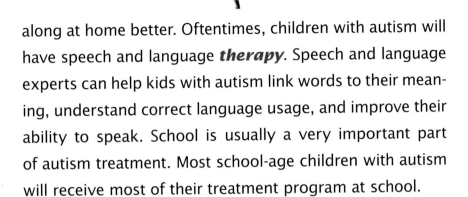

Therapy refers to many types of care and treatment for disorders and diseases.

Classifies means to put something in a certain category.

from being in the same classroom with other kids who do not have autism. In other cases, a child's autism may be so severe that she will do best in a special classroom just for kids with autism. Either way, kids with autism

39

learn best in classroom environments that remain the same from day to day. Most autistic kids dislike change, and they like routines. Kids with autism require an educational plan built to match their individual needs. This often includes learning how to talk better and how to get along with others, along with other more academic subjects like learning to read or arithmetic.

Not all kids with autism need **special education**, but many do. A law known as the Individuals with Disabilities Education Act, or IDEA, describes how schools decide which kids need special education. In order to **qualify** for IDEA, the child's condition must get in the way of him learning or taking part in school activities.

The IDEA law lists thirteen different kinds of **disabilities** that may mean a child will need special education. Autism is one **category** that falls under IDEA.

> **Special education** teaches kids who have trouble learning because of some disability.
>
> To **qualify** means to fit the definition of something or to meet the requirements.
>
> **Disabilities** are problems—either physical or mental—that get in the way of a person doing what other people can do.
>
> A **category** is a group or a certain kind of thing.

The IDEA law requires that:

- the child has problems performing well at school activities.
- the child's parent, teacher, or other school staff person must ask that the child be examined for a disability.
- the child is **evaluated** to decide if she does indeed have a disability and to figure out what kind of special education she needs.

> When something is *evaluated*, it is examined to see in which category it belongs.

- a group of people, including the kid's parents, teachers, and a school psychologist, meets to decide on a plan for helping him (or her). This plan is called an Individualized Education Program (IEP). The IEP spells out exactly what the child needs in order to succeed at school.

At the IEP meeting, parents give the school psychologist information about the child's behavior at home.

Succeeding with Autism

Parents, brothers, and sisters are also important in the life of a child with autism. They can help teach the child how to talk and get along with others. Most important, they can help the child feel loved and accepted.

Each person with autism has a different range of things she can do. Some kids with autism have amazing abilities. For example, some people with autism are excellent in math, music, and the sciences. Many kids with autism are able to focus on one complex object or task for a long period of time, where others their age may not understand or lose interest. Each person with autism is unique, with different things she can do and different things she can't.

A child with autism will not outgrow his disorder. He will have autism throughout his entire life. But many people with autism can learn to handle the challenges of their disorder. Some may grow up to have jobs that are suited to their special talents. Others will need extra help their whole life. Either way, these people are interesting individuals who are worth getting to know. In their own way, they know how to love others (even if they don't express their love the same way others do)—and they know and appreciate when they are loved and respected by others.

With the love and support.of parents, siblings, and teachers, a child with autism can learn to handle the challenges of his disorder.

If you know someone with autism, remember, it's not his fault! He can't help being the way he is, and he doesn't mean to be unfriendly or rude or unkind. He just doesn't understand things the same way you do. Making his life more difficult by teasing or bullying him will only make things worse for him. You can help build bridges between people you meet who may seem different from yourself by always treating everyone with respect, the way you would want to be treated yourself.

Further Reading

Bleach, F. *Everybody is Different: A Book for Young People Who Have Brothers or Sisters with Autism*. London, UK: The National Autistic Society, 2001.

Elder, J. *Different Like Me: My Book of Autism Heroes*. London, UK: Jessica Kingsley Publishers, 2006.

Frender, S. and R. Schiffmiller. *Brotherly Feelings: Me, My Emotions, and My Brother With Asperger's Syndrome*. Philadelphia, Penn.: Jessica Kingsley Publishers, 2007.

Keating-Velasco, J. L. *A Is for Autism, F is for Friend: A Kid's Book on Making Friends with a Child Who Has Autism*. Shawnee Mission, Kan.: Autism Asperger Publishing, 2007.

Keating-Velasco, J. L. *In His Shoes, A Short Journey Through Autism*. Shawnee Mission, Kan.: Autism Asperger Publishing, 2007.

Notbohm, E. *Ten Things Every Child with Autism Wishes You Knew*. Arlington, Tex.: Future Horizons, 2005.

Shapiro, O. *Autism and Me: Sibling Stories*. Park Ridge, Ill.: Albert Whitman, 2009.

Sicile-Kira, C. and T. Grandin. *Autism Spectrum Disorders: The Complete Guide to Understanding Autism, Asperger's Syndrome, Pervasive Developmental Disorder and Other ASDs*. New York: The Berkley Publishing Group, 2004.

Welton, J. *Can I Tell You About Asperger Syndrome?: A Guide for Friends and Family*. London, UK: Jessica Kingsley Publishers, 2004.

Willis, Clarissa. *Teaching Young Children with Autism Spectrum Disorder*. Beltsville, Ma.: Gryphon House, 2009.

Find Out More On the Internet

The ARC of the United States
www.thearc.org

Autism Research Institute
www.autism.com

Autism Society of America
www.autism-society.org

Autism Speaks
www.autismspeaks.org

The Doug Flutie, Jr. Foundation for Autism, Inc.
www.dougflutiejrfoundation.org

Families for Early Autism Treatment (FEAT)
www.feat.org

National Dissemination Center for Children with Disabilities
(NICHCY)
www.nichcy.org

Disclaimer

The websites listed on this page were active at the time of publication. The publisher is not responsible for websites that have changed their address or discontinued operation since the date of publication. The publisher will review and update the websites upon each reprint.

Index

About the Authors

Sheila Stewart has written several dozen books for young people, both fiction and nonfiction, although she especially enjoys writing fiction. She has a master's degree in English and now works as a writer and editor. She lives with her two children in a house overflowing with books, in the Southern Tier of New York State.

Camden Flath is a writer living and working in Binghamton, New York. He has a degree in English and has written several books for young people. He is interested in current political, social, and economic issues and applies those interests to his writing.

About the Consultant

Dr. Carolyn Bridgemohan is board certified in developmental behavioral pediatrics and practices at the Developmental Medicine Center at Children's Hospital Boston. She is the director of the Autism Care Program and an assistant professor at Harvard Medical School. Her specialty areas are autism and other pervasive developmental disorders, developmental and learning problems, and developmental and behavioral pediatrics.